MY FAVORITE LETTER

COLORING & ACTIVITY BOOK

A fun activity book starring Alpha Betty, the little ladybug, who is hiding somewhere on all the pages.
See if you can find her.

Possibility Lady Press
Portland, Oregon

A-MAZE-ING

Lead Betty through the maze to get from A to Z.

MAKE-A-WORD

Write down all the words you can find from the letters within these words:

MY FAVORITE LETTER

_____ _____

_____ _____

_____ _____

_____ _____

_____ _____

_____ _____

_____ _____

_____ _____

_____ _____

How many balls? ___ How many bees? ___ How many bikes? ___ Do you have a bike? ___ How many Bettys? ___ How many books? ___ Do you have the book, My Favorite Letter? ___

WORD FIND

Look up, down, across, diagonally, and backward. How many times can you find the word **CAR?**

C	A	R	C	C
A	A	R	A	A
R	C	R	R	R
R	C	C	A	C
A	R	A	C	R
C	A	R	R	A
A	C	R	A	C

Your answer: ☐

Did you color Cinderella? ___ Is Betty in a car? ___ How many cupcakes did you color? ___ Did you eat a cupcake? ___ Are you using Crayons? ___ How many? ___ How many are here? ___

CONNECT THE DOTS

Connect the dots from A to Z and then color it in!

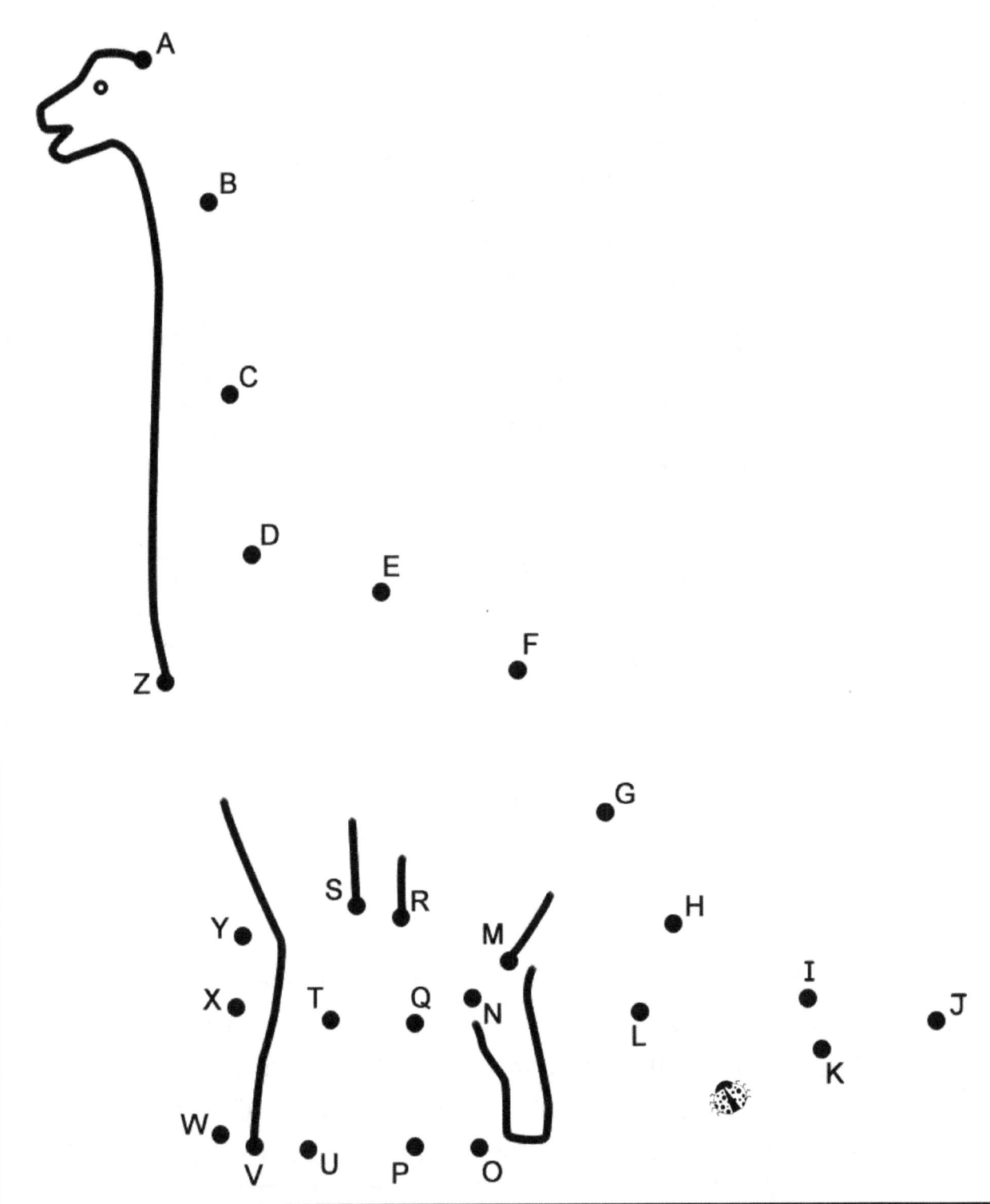

Do you see a duck? ____ Do you see a dinosaur? ____ How about a donut? ____ How many dragonflies? ____ What is Betty trying to eat? _____

MATCH 'EM!
Draw a line to connect the matching eggs!

How many Easter eggs do you count? ____ How many elves? ____ Elephants? ____ Ears? ____ What is Betty doing? _____

FOLLOW THE PATH

Follow the letters in FAIRY in order to find the correct path through the maze.

START ⬇

S	L	F	A	I	R	Y	P	A
E	F	Y	O	F	I	F	F	A
G	A	R	H	K	P	A	Y	I
M	I	I	H	I	L	I	R	R
M	R	A	A	S	N	R	I	Y
O	Y	F	C	C	U	Y	A	W
R	F	Y	R	I	A	F	F	Y
Z	A	I	R	Y	F	A	I	R

⬅ **END**

Fish, fairies, firecrackers, and Frankenstein all start with F. What are some other words that start with F? _____ _____ _____ _____ Do you see Betty? ___

CRACK THE CODE

Using the secret code below, fill in the blanks
to reveal the hidden message!

A	B	C	D	E	F	G	H	I	J	K	L	M
1	2	3	4	5	6	7	8	9	10	11	12	13
N	O	P	Q	R	S	T	U	V	W	X	Y	Z
14	15	16	17	18	19	20	21	22	23	24	25	26

__   __ __ __ __ __   __ __ __ __ __ __ __ __
9   12 15 22 5   7 15 18 9 12 12 1 19

__ __ __ __ __
7 15 1 20 19

__ __ __   __ __ __ __ __ __ __ __
1 14 4   7 9 18 1 6 6 5 19

Goodness gracious! What animals do you see here that begin with G? _____ _____ _____ How many genies are there? _____ Where is Betty hiding? _____

HOW MANY HATS?

Your Answer:

Hot diggedy dog! How many hot dogs did you color? ___ Is there a horse wearing a hat? ___ How many houses are there? ___ Is Betty in one of them? ___

IMAGINATION

Use your imagination to draw your own amazing insect!

I spy 4 things that begin with I.
What are they? _____ _____
_____ _____
Do you spy Betty? ___

WORD FIND

Look up, down, across, diagonally, and backward. How many times can you find the word **JEWEL?**

E	J	E	J	E
L	E	W	E	J
E	W	W	W	E
W	E	J	E	W
E	L	L	L	E
J	E	W	E	L

Your answer:

Just look at all the J words! Which did you color first? Jet? ___ Jar of jam? ___ Jacket? ___ Jewel? ___ Is Betty cold? ___

WORD SEARCH

Look up, down, across, diagonally, and backward.
Can you find these words?

KITE KITTEN
KAYAK KABOB
KING KEY
KOALA KANGAROO

W	K	O	K	I	T	T	E	N
B	A	E	A	Y	N	S	T	W
S	Y	E	N	B	T	O	I	O
H	A	K	G	G	N	I	K	S
W	K	N	A	T	R	A	E	H
B	E	W	R	K	A	B	O	B
K	R	T	O	L	R	H	L	I
A	L	A	O	K	B	K	I	S

Which would you rather have: a kitten or a kangaroo? _____ Would you rather be a king or a kite? What did Betty choose? _____

What 2 things give us light? _____ _____
What 2 animals are here? _____ _____
And which one does Betty like to play with?
_____

A-Maze-ing

Here are 8 little mazes.
See how quickly you can get through them!

MATCH 'EM

Draw a line to match the nests!

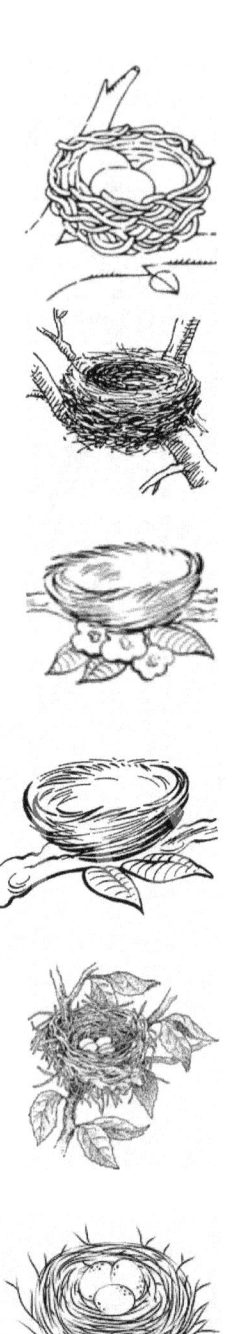

How many nests? ____ How many eggs in all the nests? ____ How many nuts? ____ How many noses? ____ How many nostrils? ____ What is Betty's favorite number? ___

WORD FIND

Look up, down, across, diagonally, and backward.
How many times can you find the word **OWL**?

O	W	L	O	L
W	O	L	W	W
L	W	O	L	O
O	W	L	L	O
O	L	W	W	W
W	O	O	O	L
L	L	W	O	O

Your answer: ☐

What are the animals on this page ? _____
_____ _____
What does Betty like to eat? _____

MAKE-A-WORD

Write down all the words you can find from the letters within the words:

PENGUIN PIG PINEAPPLE

_____   _____

_____   _____

_____   _____

_____   _____

_____   _____

_____   _____

_____   _____

_____   _____

_____   _____

_____   _____

HOW MANY QUEENS & KINGS?

What is the name of the bird that starts with Q? _____ (Hint: rhymes with mail) How many queens are here? ___ Question marks? ___ Quilts? ___ Did Betty make a quilt? ___

FOLLOW THE PATH

Follow the letters in RABBIT in order to find the correct path through the maze.

STARTS ↓

R	L	R	A	I	A	B	B	I
A	F	A	O	F	R	A	R	T
B	A	B	B	I	T	R	A	T
M	R	B	H	I	L	T	B	R
B	T	I	A	S	N	R	B	A
O	I	T	R	A	B	B	I	T	← END
R	B	Y	R	I	A	F	F	R
A	B	A	R	T	I	B	B	A

Happy faces on lots of creatures! How many rabbits? ___ How many racoons? ___ How many robots? ___ How many rockets? ___ Is Betty going to the moon? ___

CONNECT THE DOTS
And then color it in!

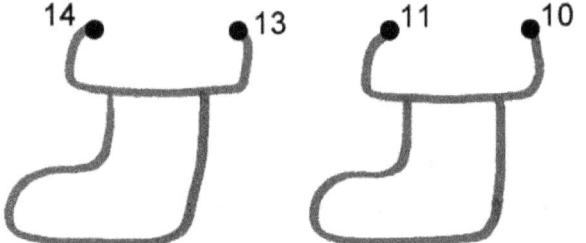

Everybody loves sunshine and Santa Claus! Do you agree? ____ Do you like snakes? ____ How about seals? ____ Betty likes them for sure!

CRACK THE CODE

Using the secret code below, fill in the blanks to reveal the hidden message!

A	B	C	D	E	F	G	H	I	J	K	L	M
1	2	3	4	5	6	7	8	9	10	11	12	13
N	O	P	Q	R	S	T	U	V	W	X	Y	Z
14	15	16	17	18	19	20	21	22	23	24	25	26

12 5 20 ' 19   18 9 4 5   9 14 1

20 18 21 3 11   20 15   20 8 5

20 18 1 9 14   19 20 1 20 9 15 14

1 14 4   7 15   15 14   1

20 18 9 16 !

What wonderful things are on this page! What do you see that starts with T? _____
_____ _____ _____ _____
What do you think Betty likes best? _____

IMAGINATION

Use your imagination to draw your own magical unicorn!

Do you love unicorns?___ How many are here? ___ Do you wear underpants? ___ How many are here? ___ Does Betty like underpants? ___ What other U things are here? _____ _____

WORD SCRAMBLE

Use the words from the list in the box
to unscramble these crazy words.

COIVE _____

CITYROV _____

NAV _____

PIMERVA _____

NIVILO _____

OCLAVON _____

NONEVIS _____

VIOLIN	VOLCANO
VAN	VOICE
VICTORY	VENISON
VAMPIRE	

Can you name a volcano? _____
Do you know someone who can play the violin? _____ Do you ever ride in a van? ____
Does Betty? ____ Are vampires real? ____

CONNECT THE DOTS

Connect the dots and then color it in!

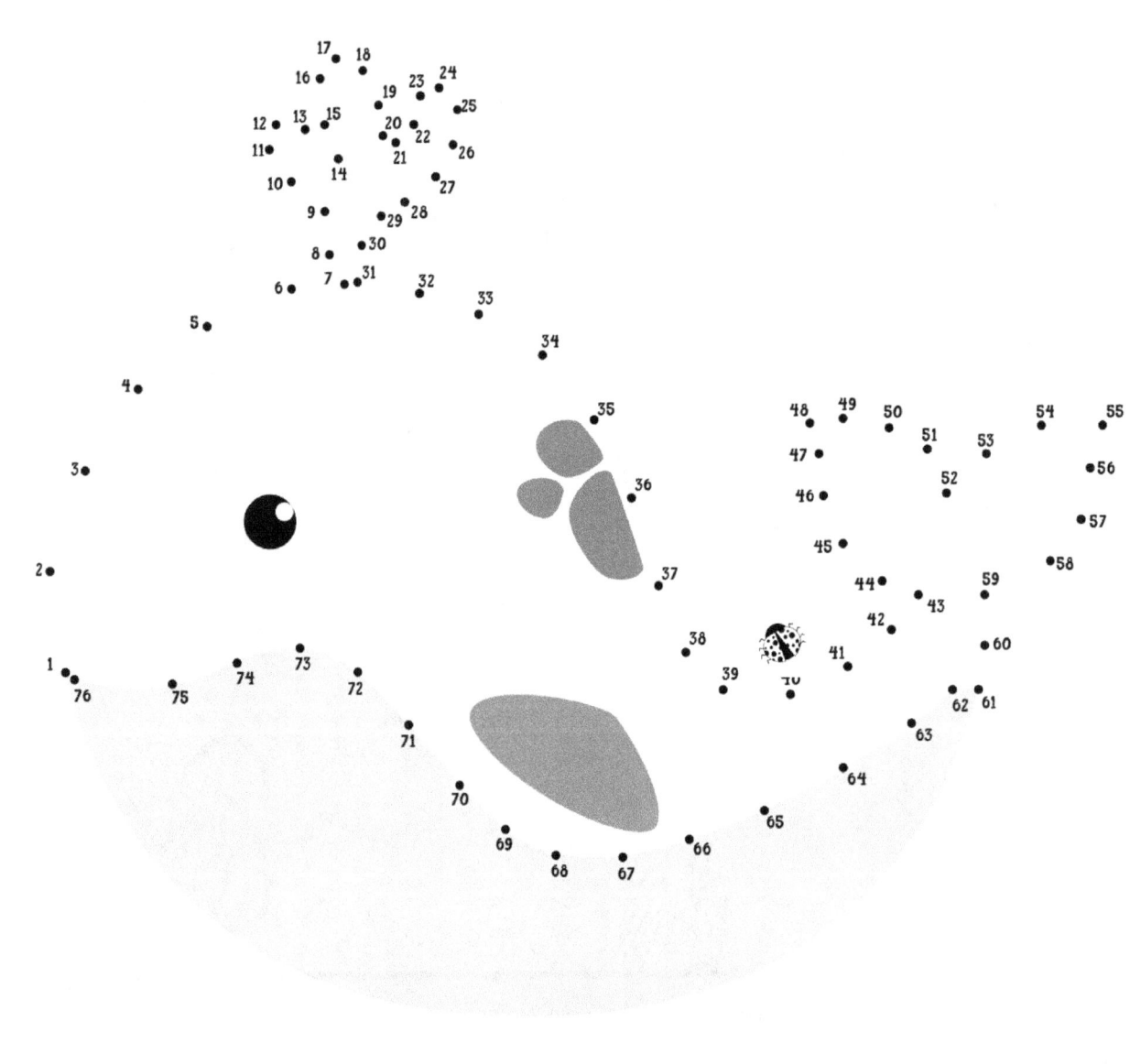

Have you ever seen a woodpecker? ___ How about a whale? ___ Do whales eat watermelon? ___ Where in the world is Betty? ___

HOW MANY HUGS (O) & KISSES (X)?

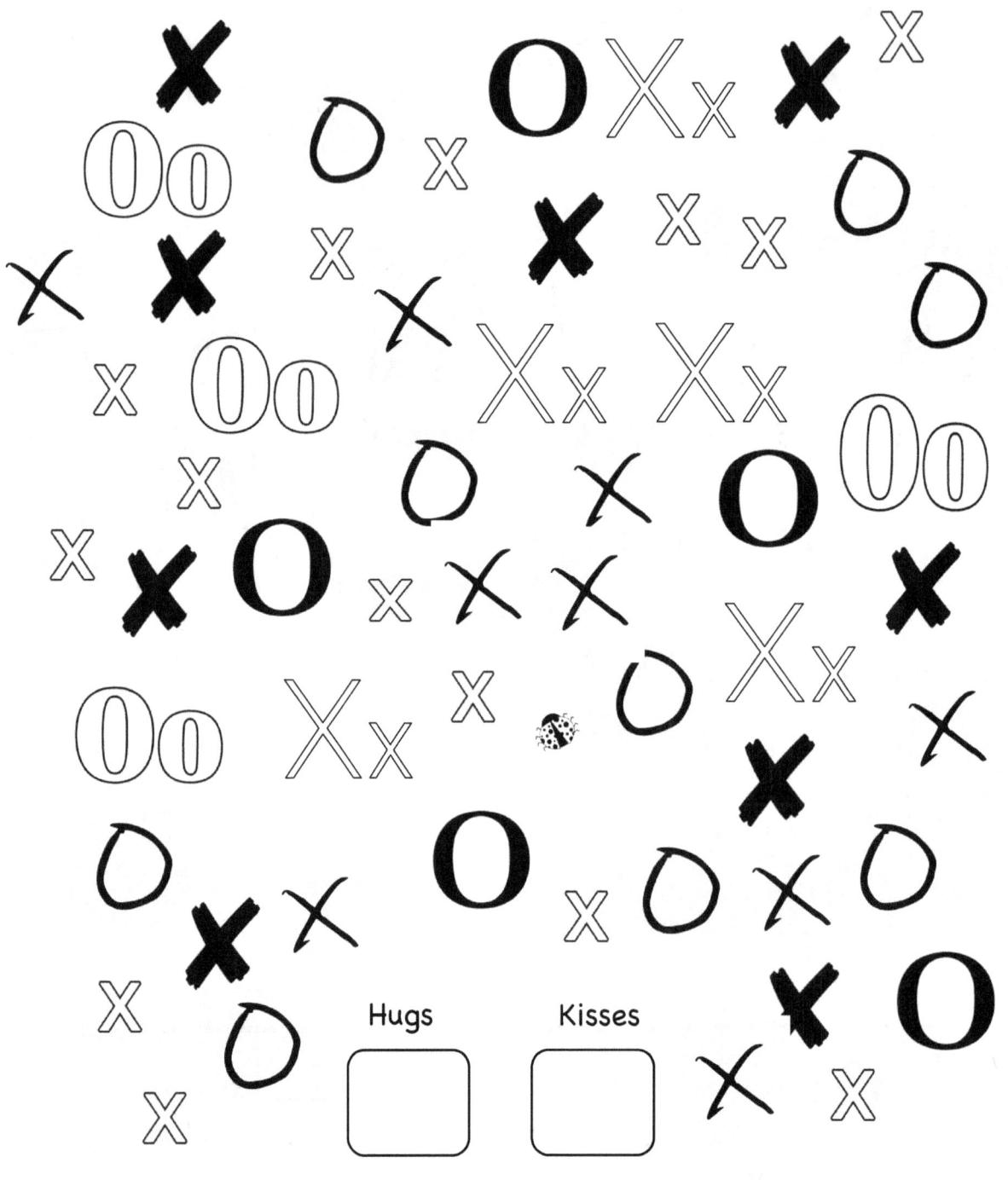

Hugs Kisses

WORD SEARCH

Look up, down, across, diagonally, and backward.
Can you find these words?

YURT   YELLOW
YARN   YAK
YOYO   YIKES
YARDS   YOU

W	E	Y	E	D	R	T	U	Y
O	S	U	O	Y	Y	Y	A	A
L	S	R	K	A	Y	R	O	R
L	W	T	Y	K	N	Y	D	D
E	Y	S	W	D	Y	U	W	S
Y	O	Y	O	W	K	O	R	Y
S	T	S	E	K	I	Y	R	D
Y	A	K	E	W	Y	K	E	S

You begins with Y and so do the things on this page. How many yardsticks are there? ____ How many yaks? ____ Yurts? ____ Yarn balls? ____ Where does Betty feel at home? _____

A-MAZE-ING

Can you find your way in and out?

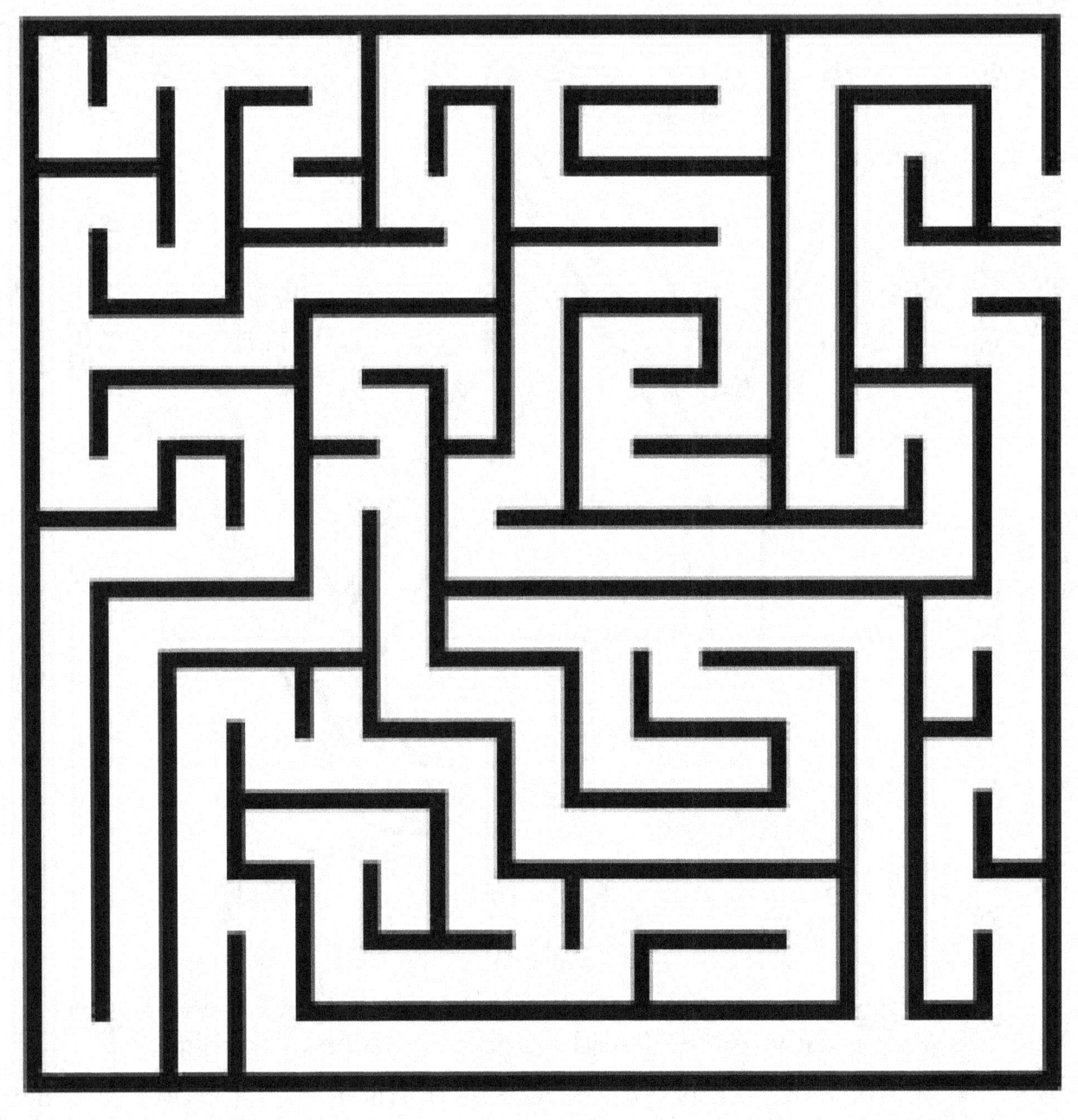

Do you think zebras like zigzags? ____ Does Betty? ____ Do zebras like to eat zucchini squash? ____ How many zippers do you see? ____

HEY, KIDS!

COME JOIN THE MFL CLUB!

We love seeing your work! Color a page from this book or complete your favorite activity. Have a grown-up take a picture of it and send it to Betty at the MFL Club headquarters. We might show it off for everyone to see!

My Favorite Letter Club

_____
Your Name

I sent my picture on _____
and now I'm a member of the MFL Club!

Upload your art to:
facebook.com/myfavoriteletter
or email it to:
myfavoriteletter909@gmail.com
Be sure to include your child's first name and age.

www.ingramcontent.com/pod-product-compliance
Lightning Source LLC
Chambersburg PA
CBHW060428010526
44118CB00017B/2400